Lucy Maud Montgomery

Jacqueline Langille

Four East Publications Ltd.
P.O. Box 29
Tantallon, Nova Scotia B0J 3J0

Copyright 1992
All rights reserved

1st printing November 1992
2nd printing July 2001

edited by Hilary Sircom
design by Paul McCormick
printing and typesetting by
    Print Atlantic
    Dartmouth, Nova Scotia, Canada

Acknowledgements

The publisher wishes to express his appreciation for the generous financial support of the **Nova Scotia Department of Tourism and Culture** and the **Canada Council**.

The Marco Polo on the front cover is courtesy of the Yarmouth County Museum and Archives. L.M. Montgomery on the front cover and the students of Prince of Wales College from the H.B. Sterling Collection c. mid 1890's, on the back cover, are courtesy of the Prince Edward Island Public Archives.

All photos used in this book are courtesy of the Prince Edward Island Public Archives, unless otherwise noted.

Richard Rogers, Publisher

Canadian Cataloguing in Publication Data
Langille, Jacqueline, 1966-

   L. M. Montgomery

   (Famous Canadians)
   Includes bibliographical references.
   ISBN 0-920427-54-5

1. Montgomery, L. M. (Lucy Maud), 1874-1942
2. Novelists, Canadian (English)—20th century—
Biography.* I. Title. II. Series: Famous
Canadians (Tantallon, N.S.)

PS8526.055275 1992   C813'.52   C92-098664-1
PR9199.3M6Z75 1992

Preface

There is for all of us a fascination in discovering how people lived in the past. Most adults are familiar with questions, "What was it like when you were growing up?" and "What did you do when you were my age?" The series is intended to address this interest and make available to young people some of the material previously found only in books directed towards the adult market. Although the biographies have been kept brief, the bibliographies will suggest reading for those who would like to do further research.

These Famous Canadians who were pioneers and innovators in their day are our local heroes and heroines; the contribution they made to our way of life is recorded in our museums and historic homes. We hope that this series will increase awareness of our Canadian heritage both for those who already live here and for the visitors who may wish to stay awhile in order to get to know us and our history better.

Hilary Sircom
General Editor

Contents

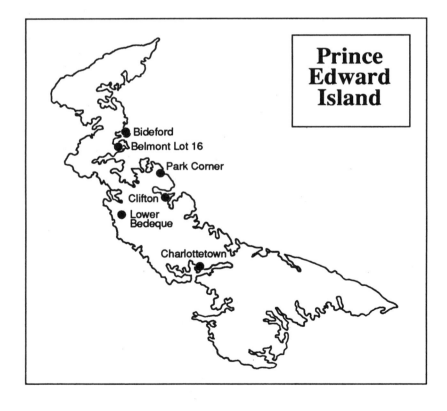

Prince Edward Island

Bideford
Belmont Lot 16
Park Corner
Clifton
Lower Bedeque
Charlottetown

Introducing Lucy Maud Montgomery 1874-1942

There are few children in North America today who have not heard of Anne of Green Gables. Most are able to recount some of the incidents in the childhood of that lovable carrot-top, but how many know anything about Lucy Maud Montgomery?

The eight books about Anne are in constant demand and have been translated into more than fifteen languages. Anne is seen in plays, movies, a ballet and on television. Tourists from around the world flock to Prince Edward Island to visit Green Gables and the other places mentioned in the stories. It seems that in this case the success of the creation overshadows the fame of the creator.

Lucy Maud Montgomery was born and brought up on Prince Edward Island and the Island people are justly proud of her. She was one of the first women in Canada to be able to make her living by writing and she led the way as a successful writer of Canadian children's fiction.

Lucy Maud was certainly not Anne or Emily or Pat or Kilmeny but by bringing a little bit of herself to each one, she made her characters come alive. Many of the incidents and places which the reader cherishes in her books were taken from L. M. Montgomery's own early life. She was a wonderful story teller who could touch with magic quite ordinary everyday happenings. Some examples of events from Lucy Maud's own childhood which appear in the stories are: the secret friends in the glass doors of the cabinet, found in <u>Anne of Green Gables</u>; the supposed coming of Judgement Day in <u>The Story Girl</u>; working in a newspaper office in the Emily books and teaching in a one-room schoolhouse in the Anne books. In addition, many tales from her own family history and from the Island's history found a place in her works.

Her dedication to writing was the force which motivated L. M. Montgomery throughout her life but she never could have imagined how popular her books would become. Her charming tales of a bygone age have been translated into countless other languages and are enjoyed today by millions of readers — both young and old alike.

Rural Prince Edward Island, ca. 1898.

Growing Up in Cavendish

Prince Edward Island was the site of the historic Charlottetown Conference of 1864, which led to the birth of the nation of Canada. A decade later another birth took place which would bring even more fame to the island province. On November 30, 1874, in the small village of Clifton Corner, P.E.I., Hugh John Montgomery, a local merchant, and his wife, Clara Woolner Macneill, became the parents of a baby girl. They named her Lucy, for her grandmother, and Maud for herself. Her family always called her Maud.

Maud's mother was not very strong and never fully recovered from the birth of her child. Before Maud was even two years old, on September 14, 1876, her mother died. Hugh Montgomery was not able to look after his infant daughter by himself, so his wife's parents, Alexander and Lucy Macneill, took Maud into their home in Cavendish.

Maud's father was often away from the island for long periods of time on business, as he worked for a shipping company. Although she missed her father, Maud enjoyed living in the large Macneill farmhouse which was surrounded by beautiful orchards and fields and was not far from the red clay sands of the wide beaches so typical of the Island.

Maud's family, the Macneills and Montgomerys, had been living on Prince Edward Island for over one hundred years. While Maud was growing up, her great-aunt, Mary

Sailing Ship, 1895.

Lawson, would tell her stories of how the first families of her ancestors had come to the island. One amusing story was of the first Montgomery to settle on P.E.I. He was Hugh Montgomery, and he had set sail from Britain with his family, intending to settle in Quebec. When the ship stopped at Prince Edward Island to take on fresh water, Hugh Montgomery's wife asked to be taken ashore for a while because she was terribly seasick. As soon as she stepped on dry land, she announced that she was staying, and no amount of pleading and begging could persuade her to go back on board. Her husband and the family had to leave the ship and start their new life on P.E.I. Maud would later use some of Great-aunt Mary's stories in her own books.

Maud's grandfather, Alexander Macneill, was the Cavendish Postmaster, and the Post Office was right in

#4 Alec MacNeill's House.

his home. It was the custom at this time in rural areas to have the Post Office in the front room of a large house. Her grandparents were busy running the farm and the Post Office, so Maud had to find ways to amuse herself. Sometimes her mother's sister, Aunt Emily, would keep her company, but when she was alone, Maud would invent secret friends to be her playmates. She would pretend that the reflection she could see of herself in the glass doors of the china cabinet was a friend. There was a different playmate in each pane of glass.

Maud grew up in a closely-knit family where there was much visiting between relatives, when the weather was fine. Often the Macneills would travel to Park Corner, about fourteen miles away, to visit Uncle John and Aunt Annie Campbell. Maud loved to go in the horse carriage to visit her favourite cousins, and looked forward to the

Horse Carriages, ca. 1911.

fun of playing with them on the Campbell farm. Her grandfather Montgomery also lived in Park Corner. He was Senator Donald Montgomery, an important political figure in P.E.I.

On one visit to Park Corner, Maud, then aged five, mistakenly picked up the wrong end of a metal poker which was used to stoke the kitchen fire. The red-hot end burned her hand very badly, and she was put straight to bed. The next day she came down with what the doctor said was typhoid fever. Whatever the cause, Maud was so ill that her family was afraid she would die. Happily in a short time she made a full recovery.

Maud learned to read when she was very young, and spent as much time as possible reading everything from newspapers and magazines, to novels and books of poetry. Even before she started school, the little girl was reading such things as Godey's <u>Lady's Book</u> and Hans Christian

Senator Donald Montgomery

Andersen's <u>Tales</u>. However, on Sundays Maud's reading was limited to what were considered to be "improving" books. Her grandparents, as strict Presbyterians, believed that on Sundays Maud should read the Bible and such works as Bunyan's "<u>Pilgrim's Progress</u>", or <u>Sermons</u> by Talmage. Her favourite story was Bulwer-Lytton's "<u>Zanoni</u>", a mystical, magical novel which she re-read in later life and still loved for its tales of enchantment and romance.

Maud had much faith in the printed words she was reading, and like other young children tended to believe everything she heard. So when she heard her grandmother reading from the newspaper one day, she listened carefully, believing every word. Her five-year-old ears were shocked by the news that the world was predicted to end next Sunday, only a few days away. Even though all the adults around her seemed to be unconcerned, Maud lived in terror until that fateful Sunday was over. When Monday dawned as usual, with the world still intact, she learned that the printed word cannot always be trusted.

When she was six years old, Maud started school. The one-room Cavendish schoolhouse was just across the road from her grandparents' farmhouse. Unless it was storming, Maud had to go home every day at lunchtime while all the other children brought their lunch in pails. Maud always had to wear shoes while the other children went barefoot in the warm weather. She hated being different and felt the other children had more fun but her grandparents had certain rules which she had to obey.

In the winter that Maud turned seven, her Aunt Emily was married. It was a big old-fashioned country wedding at the Macneill home. There was lots to eat, dancing and

Lucy Maud Montgomery at 6 years old.

Courtesy National Archives of Canada.

music, and the fun went on well into the early hours of the morning. Relatives from all around came to stay at the Macneill's, and Maud was allowed to stay up late to join in the merry-making. In spite of all the excitement, Maud was angry with Aunt Emily's new husband because he was taking her companion away and she would now often be alone in the big farmhouse.

Also that year, Maud's father moved to Saskatchewan, where he stayed for long periods working with a real estate office in developing the Canadian West. Now Maud felt really deserted. Her grandmother, wisely realizing how lonely Maud would be, decided to have two little boys come and board with the family during the next school year. At that time it was common for children from isolated areas to board with people who lived near a school. Wellington and David Nelson (known as Well and Dave) moved into the farmhouse the following summer. Well was Maud's age and Dave was a year younger.

For the next three years the children had a great deal of fun and many adventures as they explored the neighbourhood. Her two new companions shared Maud's love of nature. Together they fished, took care of pets, (one favourite kitten was named Pussy Willow), and grew their own garden. At this time Maud gave fanciful names to all the trees in the orchards around the farmhouse. The children played in the fields and forests around Cavendish, except for one small wood which they avoided because they were convinced it was haunted. After supper, they would sit on the porch and tell each other ghost stories until they were scared silly. One day, they thought for sure that they had seen a ghost, but it turned out to be only a white tablecloth which had been laid out to dry on the grass and was flapping around in the breeze.

Hugh John Montgomery, Lucy's father.

Marco Polo

The sea surrounding their Island home was always a force to be reckoned with. On July 25, 1883, the *Marco Polo* was shipwrecked on the shore off Cavendish. Maud, then aged eight, watched it all happen from the cliffs, and saw the crew and cargo being brought ashore as the ship remained foundering on the rocks. The Norwegian captain boarded with Maud's family for a short time while the rest of the crew stayed with other families in Cavendish. It was an exciting event for that quiet community and made a great impression on Maud who would write about it later on in a poem.

All Maud's reading led naturally to writing. She began to scribble on the blank backs of old letter-bills which her grandfather, the Postman, gave her. When she was nine, she wrote her first poem, entitled "Autumn," but her father, who was home at the time, said it did not sound much like poetry to him. In spite of this lack of encouragement, she even wrote poems on her slate at school when she was supposed to be doing arithmetic problems.

Maud was a leading light of the Story Club which she started with some of her school friends. The children helped each other write out wonderful romantic tales in prose and verse. Maud's vivid imagination enabled her to make something exciting out of even the quiet country life of Cavendish. Years later she would invent a heroine who had just such a vivid imagination and who would surprise her friends and acquaintances with some very tall tales.

By the time she was twelve, Maud wanted to share her poetry with the rest of the world, so she sent a poem entitled "Evening Dreams" to an American publication. The poem was rejected but Maud kept on writing in her spare time between going to school and helping with the farm chores. A year later she sent the same poem to the Charlottetown Examiner and received her second rejection. She was starting to learn the most important rule for an aspiring author: "Never give up!"

When she was fifteen, she wrote about the Marco Polo shipwreck that she had witnessed seven years before. Her poem placed third for Queens County, P.E.I. in the Canada Prize Competition of 1890. Maud was also gaining recognition for her speaking abilities, as she participated in school recitals. She was no longer a shy, withdrawn little girl; instead she was becoming a talented, confident young woman.

Prince Edward Island train station, 1895.

Young Woman: New Experiences

Maud's father was now living in Saskatchewan; he had remarried in 1887 and made a home for his new wife in Prince Albert. In 1890 he invited Maud to come and live with them. She left P.E.I. on her first train ride accompanied by her grandfather, Senator Donald Montgomery. They arrived at their destination on August 22nd, probably travelling the last miles by wagon as the railway lines were not connected all the way to Prince Albert until later that summer.

Maud found the town attractive as it lay nestled in a forested valley with the river passing by. She settled into the family home ready to begin a new life and was enrolled in the Prince Albert high school. However, despite her best intentions, she was very homesick. Her stepmother constantly needed her help with the household duties and in looking after her young half-sister and later a baby half-brother. Her father was frequently absent as he was working as a fisheries officer, Justice of the Peace, forest ranger and land speculator. The terrible weather of a Saskatchewan winter was a new and unpleasant experience. All these things combined to make Maud long for her Island home.

Although she had no opportunity for fun with young people of her own age, Maud did manage to keep on with her writing; life in Prince Albert was made bearable by the small literary successes she had at this time. On November 26th 1890, the Charlottetown Daily Patriot

Silver Bush, Park Corner.

#2320/38-8

printed her poem about the Cape Le Force legend, in which a French sea captain was killed in a duel and buried on the Cape near Cavendish. Maud was so happy to finally see her work in print! Then in the winter a poem was printed in the Montreal Witness and the following June her essay about Saskatchewan called "A Western Eden" appeared in the Prince Albert Times.

In the summer of 1891, Hugh Montgomery, concerned for his daughter's happiness, brought Maud back to P.E.I. For the rest of his life, he kept in touch by letters, but only a few short visits brought father and daughter together. Maud missed her father but P.E.I. was her home and she realized that his life now was with his new family in Saskatchewan. She spent that winter in Park Corner, living with relatives, and giving music lessons, continuing to write and send poems to the Patriot.

Prince of Wales College, Charlottetown, 1894.

The fall of 1892 saw Maud back at school in Cavendish to prepare for the entrance examination to Prince of Wales College in Charlottetown. She needed to study hard for she wanted to become a teacher. Few jobs were open to women in the late nineteenth century, and Maud did not think she could earn her living by writing as she had never yet been paid for any of her work. By being a teacher she might become independent.

When she was young, going to "Town" had been a great event, something to look forward to during the long winter months, as it meant quite an expedition by carriage from Cavendish. Now, having passed the examination, Maud spent a year in Charlottetown, the Island's capital. While there she received her first "payment" for a poem when an American magazine sent her two free subscriptions and printed "Only a Violet".

Staff of Prince of Wales College, ca. 1894.

This was encouraging and she persevered with her writing, determined that one day she would write something of enduring value by which she would be remembered.

Maud Montgomery graduated with her Second Class Teacher's Certificate in 1894, so she spent the following school year teaching at Bideford, P.E.I. She boarded at a farmhouse in Bideford and, as she was so busy teaching, she would get up an hour earlier every morning in order to write in the cold kitchen, all wrapped up in blankets. Only a really dedicated writer would get up at six o'clock in the middle of winter to work by lamplight.

After teaching for a year, on July 23, 1895, Maud received her First Class Licence, but she decided to take a special course before going back to work. That autumn

Lower Bedeque schoolhouse.

#2320/38-10

she enrolled at Dalhousie College in Halifax (now Dalhousie University) to take a course in English literature from Professor Archibald MacMechan. This was the winter of her "Big Week" when she received three separate payments for her writings totalling $22.00! She now felt rich and used the money to buy books of poetry.

The next two years were spent teaching in P.E.I., first at Belmont Lot 16, then in Lower Bedeque. She wrote all this time, mostly pieces for Sunday School publications and some children's stories. While working hard at her writing, at the same time she was becoming a good school teacher. It seemed that now she would certainly be able to support herself.

Lucy Maud Montgomery at age 19.

Duty Calls

In March 1898, Maud's Grandfather Macneill passed away, so she returned to Cavendish to be with her grandmother. Lucy Macneill became the Postmistress, taking on her husband's duties, and Maud became her assistant, also helping with the chores around the house. Uncle John, whose house was on the same land, ran the farm after his father's death. Maud had to give up teaching, but she never stopped writing, and the payments she was receiving from papers and magazines began to make her a reasonable income. Another sadness occurred soon after; her father died in Prince Albert in January, 1900. They had not been close for some years, but Maud would miss her father all the rest of her life.

Grandmother Macneill was managing well so, after a couple years, Maud decided to try something new. She promised to return if her grandmother should need her. In the fall of 1901, she moved to Halifax, Nova Scotia to join the staff of the Halifax newspaper the Daily Echo. Never had she been so busy; she was proofreading, editing, writing on demand, and doing all the odd jobs that no one else would do. She had such long days, and was so tired at night, that she had to find extra minutes while at work during the day to do her own writing. She was writing "pot-boilers" for various magazines, where the plot was given to her and she filled in the details. She did not enjoy doing this, but the work was well paid. These "pot-boilers" also began to earn her recognition, and she began to receive fan letters. Maud always made a point of answering every fan letter herself. Working at the Daily Echo was a good experience; she learned how to write

Lucy Maud Montgomery, on left, with friends in P.E.I.

under pressure and in any spare moment. Although nine out of ten of her manuscripts were rejected the first time they were mailed away to publishers, she had certainly learned not to give up.

As well as answering her fan mail, Maud started writing to a number of pen pals. In March 1902, she received her first letter from Ephraim Weber, a bachelor homesteader from Alberta, who would become a lifelong friend. Weber was an amateur writer who admired the work of L. M. Montgomery which he had read in several American magazines. He had mistakenly assumed L. M. Montgomery was a man and was most surprised to learn her true identity. Another special friendship developed through correspondence with George Boyd McMillan, a journalist living in Alloa, Clackmannanshire, Scotland. Maud enjoyed writing to other people who had literary ambitions and valued these friendships as there were few people with her own interests in the small village of Cavendish. She liked to correspond with "kindred spirits".

In June of 1902, Maud returned to the Cavendish farmhouse to stay with her grandmother as she had promised. Her life became filled with the daily chores of a typical farmhouse: cooking, cleaning, sewing and gardening. Maud most enjoyed the gardening for then she was close to nature and the beautiful island scenery she loved. She liked growing many different kinds of flowers.

Life in Cavendish may have been quiet but it was not boring. Maud took occasional holidays away from home and often visited her favourite cousins in Park Corner. She was always involved in the community as church organist, Sunday School teacher and a member of the Cavendish Literary Society. She enjoyed the country pursuits, taking long walks, bathing at Cavendish beach, taking photographs and collecting souvenirs on the shore to send to her pen friends.

Maud was still selling her work quite regularly and was now making a name for herself in the North American serial market. She was making a comfortable living; in 1903 she earned $500, a considerable sum for those days; in 1904 $591.85 and in 1906 more than $700. By now she had been published in almost every magazine in North America, but she yearned to write something more important, like a book.

Finally, in the spring of 1904, she started work on a simple idea and began her book which she called <u>Anne of Green Gables</u>. She typed out the manuscript on an old typewriter which hardly worked and when it was finished in October of the next year, sent it off to a publisher. Five publishing companies in turn rejected her book, so she put it in a hat box and hid it in a closet.

A year earlier, a new minister had come to the Cavendish Presbyterian Church, a pleasant young man named Ewan Macdonald, who had been born and raised on the island. Maud had attracted her first sweetheart when she was twelve and there had been a few other romances, but she felt something special for the Reverend Ewan Macdonald.In 1906 they secretly became engaged to be married. He was on his way to Scotland, and Maud had to stay with her grandmother, but they promised to wait for each other, no matter how far they were separated over the next few years.

Success At Last

One day, while cleaning out a closet, Maud found her old <u>Anne of Green Gables</u> manuscript and decided to give it one more try. She re-typed it and sent it to L.C. Page and Company, a publisher in Boston. On April 8, 1907, L.C. Page accepted <u>Anne of Green Gables</u> and Maud agreed to sell them the manuscript on a royalty basis. She felt that finally she was on her way to literary success, but she would have been amazed if she could have known just how popular her book for girls would become.

On June 20, 1908, Maud received her own printed copy of <u>Anne of Green Gables</u>, and over the following months, this book took its author and the world by surprise. It was an instant success, selling thousands of copies all over the English-speaking world. Even Mark Twain, the celebrated American author wrote to Maud, praising the merits of <u>Anne</u> in the realm of children's fiction. L.M. Montgomery became a star, with fan mail pouring in and a huge royalty check for $1,730 arriving in February, 1909. Soon people wanted a sequel, so Maud went to work. <u>Anne of Avonlea</u> was published in 1909, and was equally successful.

Maud wrote and published two more books in the next two years. She became a celebrity almost over night; meeting famous people like the Governor General of Canada, Earl Grey, and travelling to Boston became normal parts of her new life as a successful author. In spite of the success for which she had worked so hard not everything was happy in Maud's life. Her favourite great-aunt, Mary Lawson, died in 1909, and her grandmother, Lucy Macneill, passed away in 1911, at the age of 86. She had been the only mother Maud had ever known.

After his mother's death, Uncle John took over the farm and Maud moved into his house at Park Corner. Here, at last, after an engagement of five years, on July 5th 1911, Ewan Macdonald and Lucy Maud Montgomery were married.

Ewan took his bride on a three month honeymoon tour of England and Scotland. They enjoyed stopping at all the places of historical interest and admired the charm of the old world, the home of their ancestors. However, for Maud the highlight of the trip was the meeting with her long-time pen pal, George MacMillan who acted as their guide as they toured Scotland. It was a memorable trip but the couple were glad to come back home to Canada.

Reverend Ewan Macdonald was serving in the parish of Leaksdale, Ontario, so Maud Macdonald started married life far away from her beloved Prince Edward Island. However, she brought all her things from the Island to fill her new home; she also brought an important member of her family to live with them, Daffy the Cavendish cat. Cats had always been special friends to Maud, and she would love them throughout her life.

In spite of the publicity her books had created, Maud was a reserved person, but she knew that the people of the Leaksdale parish would look to her for guidance as the minister's wife. She opened her heart and home to the people of that small Ontario town. Her husband did well as the minister there, and the Macdonalds were an important part of the community. Maud was involved in all the church groups, working hard to support her husband's ministry.

World War I troops marching.

Life became even busier when the Macdonald's first son, Chester Cameron, was born in July, 1912. Now Maud had even less time for writing, but she hired housekeepers, and became good at doing two things at once, like plotting out a story and darning socks. She continued to write and be published, even when her second son, Ewan Stuart, was born in October, 1915. (Another baby boy had been stillborn in 1914).

When World War One started in 1914, Maud was greatly troubled by the horrors and suffering she read about in the newspapers. Also, about this time, she discovered that her husband was not well. Ewan would suffer from a nervous ailment for the rest of his life, becoming a great burden to Maud, as she looked after him. Worried about the fighting in Europe and about her

31

*Portrait of Lucy Maud Montgomery in her late thirties,
in evening dress.*

husband, Maud began to regard her dreams as omens of what would happen in the war. She helped with the Red Cross war effort, and continued to go on lecture tours, but she was in a nervous state for much of the time. By 1918, her spirit needed a time of renewal, so she spent six weeks in P.E.I. A summer in her home province was always a good tonic, and by the fall, she also had the relief of knowing that the war was over.

In 1916, Maud had ended her business relationship with L.C. Page, her original publisher, but she would continue to have problems with the company for many years. A silent movie was produced from <u>Anne of Green Gables</u> in 1919, but Maud received no money from the film because her original contract had not mentioned movie rights; few movies were being made in 1907 when the original contract was signed. When Page published an unauthorized selection of short stories in 1920, Maud knew her rights had been violated, so she took L.C. Page to court. She sued them for the royalties from her stories in a court case that lasted for nine years, and took her to Boston several times to testify.

The Macdonalds were involved in another court case in 1920 when Ewan had an automobile accident. He had never been a good driver even of the horse and buggy, and he proved to be worse when they bought their first car in 1918. He ran into a Methodist preacher's car and lost the case which was brought against him. In spite of legal battles, life went on as usual at the Leaksdale Manse. The Campbell cousins from P.E.I. would come to visit; Maud was involved with youth groups in the community and she also directed amateur theatrical companies. She was always busy, but even when she had to look after Ewan when he had one of his "spells", no one heard Mrs.

MacKay automobile, ca. 1913.

Macdonald complain. Sometimes she would tell her pen friends about the ups and downs of her life, but she always kept a calm face for the parishioners.

Maud was further honoured in 1923 when she became the first Canadian woman to be made a Fellow of the Royal Society of Arts in England. She was always in demand to give readings from her work and she enjoyed travelling on lecture tours. It amazed Maud that adults from all walks of life, as well as children, were reading and enjoying her books. In 1927, the British Prime Minister, Stanley Baldwin, wanted to meet her when he was visiting P.E.I. because he had read all her books. Later she was presented to HRH the Prince of Wales and his brother, who both respected her success as an author.

Maud was honoured to meet all these famous people, but she was more excited about finally meeting her long

Lucy Maud Montgomery, front row center, with the Norval theatrical society.

---

time pen friend, Ephraim Weber in July, 1928. They visited together only three times but their friendship spanned the miles between, and they continued to correspond until the time of Maud's death.

When he was old enough, Maud sent her eldest son, Chester, to board at St. Andrew's School in Toronto. A year later, the whole family moved when Ewan accepted a post at the Norval Continuing Presbyterian Church. Maud brought her talents as a minister's wife with her to Norval, Ontario, where she continued to direct plays and become involved in the community life of the church. Stuart was sent to join his brother at St. Andrew's in September, 1928, because Maud wanted to make sure her boys received a quality education.

The next year was unhappy for Maud as she was quite ill, missed her sons terribly, and Ewan had another car accident. Throughout all her troubles, Maud continued to write stories full of humour and with happy endings, never letting her readers see the pain her real life sometimes caused her. The boys did well in school, with Stuart becoming junior gymnastic champion of Ontario for two years before winning the national title at the Canadian National Exhibition in September, 1933. That fall, Stuart entered the University of Toronto to study medicine, while his brother was studying engineering. Maud and Ewan could be justly proud of their children.

The MacDonald family, Maud and her husband Ewan and their sons Stuart, left, and Chester, right.

Retirement from the Ministry

When Ewan retired from the ministry in 1935, the Macdonalds moved to Toronto so that their sons could live at home while they attended university. The 1930's were the years of the Great Depression and many people in North America were experiencing hard times. The Macdonald family was comfortably off because of the earnings from Maud's books, and Maud was glad to be able to help in the relief efforts for those who were less fortunate. She was always willing to give of herself to help those in need.

Finally in 1929, the court case against L.C. Page Company had been decided in her favour, but she still did not have any motion picture rights. In 1936, another movie was produced based on the <u>Anne of Green Gables</u> story, and this time it was a "talkie". Anne would always be a favourite with the public, in books, in movies, and in the plays and musicals to come.

Through all her years of troubles, with court cases, accidents, sickness, and Ewan's melancholy, Maud's writing spirit triumphed. She published eight books between 1926 and 1936, none of which betrayed her inner sorrows. More honours were to come, and in 1935, she was invested with the Order of the British Empire by the Governor General, Lord Bessborough. The Canadian government wanted to preserve the areas around Cavendish as a national park. At first, Maud did not like the idea of the general public wandering through the

Governor General of Canada, Lord Bessborough.

Signed portrait of Lucy Maud Montgomery in 1935.

Courtesy National Archives of Canada.

forests and meadows where she had spent her childhood. Then she realized that the government would save these precious places from destruction, and that it was a great honour to have people want to visit P.E.I. because of her books.

Other people continued to be inspired by L.M. Montgomery's writings, and in 1937, two plays were written based on the Anne stories. They were hits in Canada and eventually were performed around the world. Maud herself continued to write, producing Jane of Lantern Hill in 1937 and the last Anne book, Anne of Ingleside, in 1938 (published in 1939). This was to be the last book she finished.

During the last years of her life Maud was unwell, suffering from nervous breakdowns in both 1938 and 1940, and she was depressed by having to take care of her increasingly ill husband for longer periods of time. She was also greatly upset by the outbreak of World War Two in 1939. Although neither of her sons had to serve in the Canadian forces, the problems of the world weighed heavily upon her.

Maud's two pen friends knew she was not doing well because now she rarely wrote to them. No longer did Weber or MacMillan receive the seventeen-page or longer epistles they were accustomed to; Maud only had the energy to write a few lines on a postcard. She often complained in these notes of not feeling well, of not enjoying her life, of how much she missed her island paradise.

Finally her burdens became too much, and on April 24, 1942, L.M. Montgomery died at the age of sixty-seven. Her husband and two sons took her to P.E.I. for one last time and laid her to rest at Cavendish, the home of her heart.

Lucy Maud Montgomery MacDonald's gravesite.

#2320/38-11

At the funeral, her poem called "The Watchman" was read. A great many people attended to mourn the passing of one of the Island's greatest daughters, and one of Canada's best-loved authors. Her husband, Ewan Macdonald was buried beside her in December, 1943.

Lucy Maud Montgomery

From Past to Present

Perhaps L.M. Montgomery's greatest monument is found in the enduring quality of her work; children and adults for many generations to come will read and enjoy her books (24 in all between 1908 and 1939). As a young girl, Maud had said she wanted to do something great in literature, and this she did by firmly establishing the excellence of Canadian children's literature, by becoming self-sufficient through her pen, and by creating a lovable character in Anne of Green Gables who will live forever in the hearts of her readers.

Other memorials exist to honour one of Canada's favourite daughters: the Prince Edward Island National Park preserves Maud's childhood haunts for all the world to visit. The golf course at Cavendish has as its final hole "The Montgomery"; one of the Canadian National ferries which plies the strait between P.E.I. and the mainland is named the *Lucy Maud Montgomery*. In May, 1975, Canada Post issued a stamp with Lucy Maud Montgomery and a picture of Anne of Green Gables on it; Montgomery Hall is a residence at the school which used to be called Prince of Wales College, in Charlottetown. An *Anne of Green Gables* musical is performed every year at the Charlottetown festival, drawing an audience from all over the world; the Canadian Broadcasting Corporation made a movie for television about Anne. It was so popular that they made a sequel, and also developed a weekly television series called "Road to Avonlea". In Japan,

Green Gables, Provincial Park.

#2320/38-9

where Anne has a tremendous following, a replica of Green Gables is being built in order to try to stem the yearly exodus of Japanese fans to Canada.

Lucy Maud Montgomery's stories come to us as a breath of fresh Prince Edward Island air. One thinks that she would be happy to know that in a world which becomes increasingly materialistic and sophisticated, Anne has become a symbol of all that is fresh, honest and uncomplicated.

Lucy Maud Montgomery in a field of daisies, 1930s.

#2320/38-3

Books by
L. M. Montgomery

(in order of publication date)
Anne of Green Gables, L. C. Page & Co.,
Boston, 1908
Anne of Avonlea, L. C. Page & Co., Boston,
1909
Kilmeny of the Orchard, L. C. Page & Co.,
Boston, 1910
The Story Girl, L. C. Page & Co., Boston,
1911
Chronicles of Avonlea, L. C. Page & Co.,
Boston, 1912
The Golden Road, L. C. Page & Co., Boston,
1913
Anne of the Island, L. C. Page & Co., Boston,
1915
The Watchman & Other Poems, McClelland
& Stewart, Toronto, 1916
Anne's House of Dreams, Frederick Stokes &
Co., New York, 1919
Rainbow Valley, Frederick Stokes & Co.,
New York, 1919
Further Chronicles of Avonlea, L. C. Page &
Co., Boston, 1920

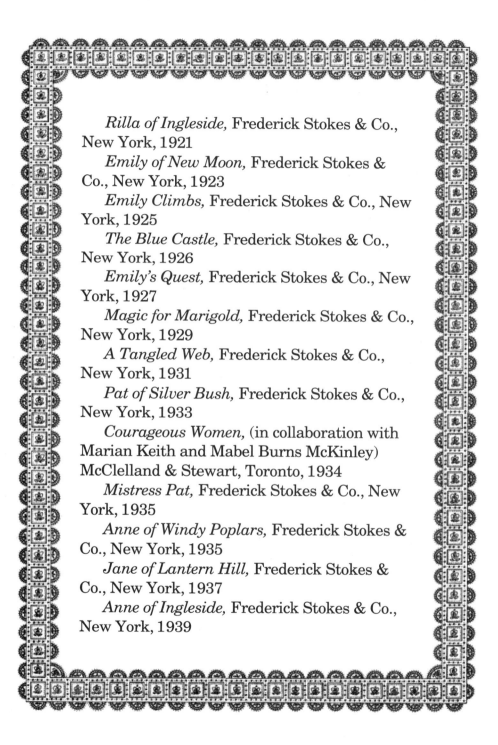

Rilla of Ingleside, Frederick Stokes & Co., New York, 1921

Emily of New Moon, Frederick Stokes & Co., New York, 1923

Emily Climbs, Frederick Stokes & Co., New York, 1925

The Blue Castle, Frederick Stokes & Co., New York, 1926

Emily's Quest, Frederick Stokes & Co., New York, 1927

Magic for Marigold, Frederick Stokes & Co., New York, 1929

A Tangled Web, Frederick Stokes & Co., New York, 1931

Pat of Silver Bush, Frederick Stokes & Co., New York, 1933

Courageous Women, (in collaboration with Marian Keith and Mabel Burns McKinley) McClelland & Stewart, Toronto, 1934

Mistress Pat, Frederick Stokes & Co., New York, 1935

Anne of Windy Poplars, Frederick Stokes & Co., New York, 1935

Jane of Lantern Hill, Frederick Stokes & Co., New York, 1937

Anne of Ingleside, Frederick Stokes & Co., New York, 1939

Bibliography

Bolger, Francis W.P. *The Years Before "Anne"*. P.E.I.: The Prince Edward Island Heritage Foundation, 1975.

Gillen, Mollie. *Lucy Maud Montgomery*. Toronto: Fitzhenry Ltd., 1978.

Gillen, Mollie. *The Wheel of Things*. London: George G. Harrap & Co. Ltd., 1976.

Lucy Maud Montgomery, *The Island's Lady of Stories*. Springfield, P.E.I.: The Women's Institute, 1963.

Montgomery, L.M. *The Alpine Path*. Toronto: Fitzhenry & Whiteside Ltd., 1974.

Ridley, Hilda M. *The Story of L.M. Montgomery*. Toronto: The Ryerson Press, 1956.